鳥　山　明

My son is five months old now, and he's very healthy and active. However, my cat, Koge, is not doing as well. I guess Koge feels that he has a new rival. Before my son was born, Koge never wanted much attention from us, but now he's all over us. Koge goes out of his way to sleep in Sasuke's blanket, and when I am holding Sasuke, Koge will try to cuddle or get me to pick him up. Can't we all just get along?

–*Akira Toriyama, 1987*

Artist/writer Akira Toriyama burst onto the manga scene in 1980 with the wildly popular **Dr. Slump**, a science fiction comedy about the adventures of a mad scientist and his android "daughter." In 1984 he created his hit series **Dragon Ball**, which ran until 1995 in Shueisha's bestselling magazine **Weekly Shonen Jump**, and was translated into foreign languages around the world. Since **Dragon Ball**, he has worked on a variety of short series, including **Cowa!**, **Kajika**, **Sand Land**, and **Neko Majin**, as well as a children's book, **Toccio the Angel**. He is also known for his design work on video games, particularly the **Dragon Warrior** RPG series. He lives with his family in Japan.

DRAGON BALL VOL. 9
The SHONEN JUMP Manga Edition

This volume is number 9 in a series of 42.

STORY AND ART BY
AKIRA TORIYAMA
ENGLISH ADAPTATION BY
GERARD JONES

Translation/Mari Morimoto
Touch-Up Art & Lettering/Wayne Truman
Cover Design/Sean Lee & Dan Ziegler
Graphics & Design/Sean Lee
Senior Editor/Jason Thompson

Printed in Canada

In the original Japanese edition, DRAGON BALL and DRAGON BALL Z are known collectively as the 42-volume series DRAGON BALL. The English DRAGON BALL Z was originally volumes 17-42 of the Japanese DRAGON BALL.

Published by VIZ Media, LLC
P.O. Box 77010 • San Francisco, CA 94107

SHONEN JUMP Manga Edition
10 9 8 7 6 5
First printing, May 2003
Fifth printing, August 2011

www.viz.com

PARENTAL ADVISORY
DRAGON BALL is rated T for Teen. It may contain violence, language, alcohol or tobacco use, or suggestive situations. It is recommended for ages 13 and up.
ratings.viz.com

www.shonenjump.com

SHONEN JUMP MANGA

DRAGON BALL

Vol. 9

DB: 9 of 42

STORY AND ART BY
AKIRA TORIYAMA

THE MAIN CHARACTERS

Son Goku

Monkey-tailed young Goku has always been stronger than normal. His grandfather Gohan gave him the *nyoibô*, a magic staff, and Kame-Sen'nin gave him the *kinto'un*, a magic flying cloud.

Bulma

A genius inventor, Bulma met Goku on her quest for the seven magical Dragon Balls.

Yamcha

Yamcha used to be a desert bandit, but he went to the city to be Bulma's on-and-off boyfriend. He uses "Fist of the Wolf-Fang" kung-fu.

Lunch

A strange woman whose personality changes whenever she sneezes.

Kuririn

Goku's former martial arts school-mate under Kame-Sen'nin.

The All-Seeing Crone

The All-Seeing Crone

Also known as "Baba Uranai" or "Fortuneteller Baba," this old witch can see the future and locate anything, but her services don't come cheap.

Upa

Pu'ar

Yamcha's shapeshifting friend.

Pu'ar

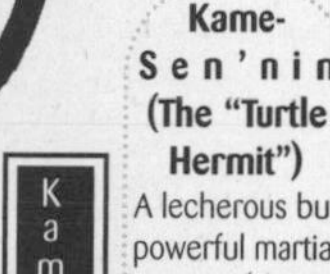

Pilaf and Co.

Upa

A young boy who lived with his father Bora in the area around the Karin Tower. When the Red Ribbon Army killed Upa's father, Goku vowed to gather the Dragon Balls and wish his father back to life.

Kame-Sen'nin (The "Turtle Hermit")

Kame-Sen'nin

A lecherous but powerful martial artist (also known as the *muten-rôshi*, or "Invincible Old Master") who trained Goku's grandfather, Son Gohan, as well as Goku himself. He taught Goku the *kamehameha* attack.

Pilaf and Co.

A little emperor who wants to get the Dragon Balls so he can wish to rule the entire world.

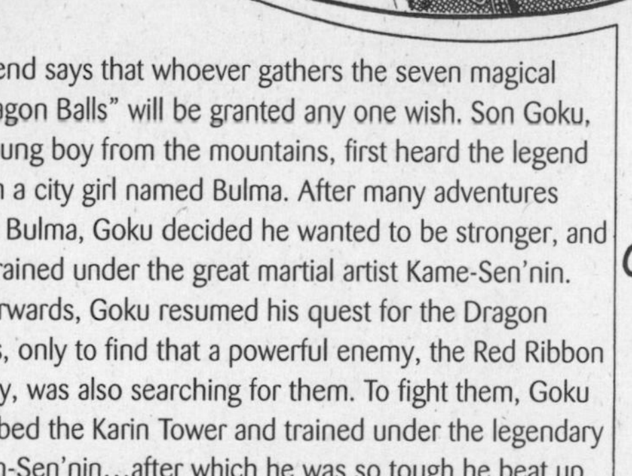

Legend says that whoever gathers the seven magical "Dragon Balls" will be granted any one wish. Son Goku, a young boy from the mountains, first heard the legend from a city girl named Bulma. After many adventures with Bulma, Goku decided he wanted to be stronger, and so trained under the great martial artist Kame-Sen'nin. Afterwards, Goku resumed his quest for the Dragon Balls, only to find that a powerful enemy, the Red Ribbon Army, was also searching for them. To fight them, Goku climbed the Karin Tower and trained under the legendary Karin-Sen'nin…after which he was so tough he beat up everyone at Red Ribbon Army HQ all by himself!

DRAGON BALL 9

Tale 97 • The Lost Dragon Ball

ASTOUNDINGLY, SON GOKU MANAGED TO DECIMATE THE RED RIBBON ARMY SINGLE-HANDEDLY--AND ONLY HAS ONE DRAGON BALL LEFT TO FIND! HOWEVER...

THIS IS IT!! THE STRONGHOLD OF OUR ULTIMATE ENEMY!!
CAPSULE CORP.

LET'S TAKE IT DOWN !!
WHY ARE WE LANDING SO FAR AWAY? IT'S WAY OVER THERE.

IF WE GET TOO CLOSE, THEY'LL SHOOT US DOWN! WE'LL BE USELESS THEN!
HYUUUUN
WE'VE GOT TO RUSH THE PLACE WITHOUT BEING SEEN FIRST!

H-HERE GOES NOTHING.. !
LET'S GET GOKU OUT OF THERE !
CAPSUL CORP

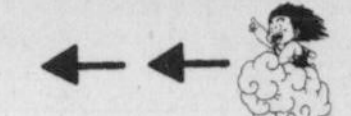

WAIT! WE CAN'T JUST CHARGE INTO THE PLACE WITH NO PLAN!
WE NEED A STRATEGY!
OH YEAH...

GOOD LUCK, YOU GUYS!! I KNOW YOU'LL BEAT THEM!!
DON'T YOU MEAN "WE"?!!!

B-BUT I HAVE A STOMACH ACHE!! OW-WEEEE!!
AND I SUPPOSE YOU HAVE A NOTE FROM YOUR MOTHER?!!
...

AS THE OLD SAYING GOES, WE'RE SO BUSY WE'D EVEN ASK FOR HELP FROM A PIG!!
THAT'S SUPPOSED TO BE "A CAT"!!!!

ARRGH!
THAT STUPID GOKU WOULD GET ME INTO THIS...!

HEY!! SHUT YOUR YELLOW-BELLIED TRAPS AND LET'S START KICKING BUTT!!
TH-THIS PERSON... IS A WOMAN, RIGHT...?

BLAH BLAH BLAH
BUZZ BUZZ BUZZ
...THEN IF BULMA TAKES OFF HER CLOTHES AND DISTRACTS THE SOLDIERS.....
YOU'VE GOT TO BE KIDDING ME!!
NO TO THIS, NO TO THAT

ALL RIGHT, THEN WHY DON'T I ATTACK FROM THE LEFT...
HUH ?

EVERY-BODY, DOWN!! SOME-THING'S COMIN' AT US !!
WHAT ?!

WAAH-- !!
CURSES!! OUR PLANE WILL BE SPOTTED!!
CAPSULE CORP.

RETURN IT TO CAPSULE FORM !!
YES, MA'AM !!

PIIP

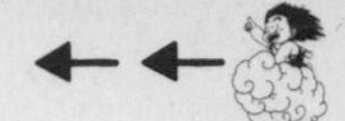

POP

PHEW
!
LET'S HOPE WE HAVEN'T BEEN DISCOVERED....

HUH...
?

ISN'T THAT....
?!
IT IS!! IT'S GOKU!!

FOOEY!! THAT DUMB DRAGON RADAR BROKE AGAIN...
I'VE GOT TO GO BACK TO THE TURTLE GUY'S HOUSE AND GET BULMA TO FIX IT... BUT I DON'T KNOW HOW TO GET THERE FROM HERE...

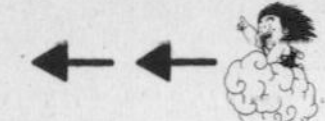

GOKU--
!!!
YO!!
GOKU--
!!
HEY--
OVER
HERE--
!!!
PHEW...
HE'S
STILL
ALIVE...

HUH
?
GOKU--
DOWN
HERE--!

WHA--
?!
GOKU!
GOKU--!

HYUUUUN
YOU
GUYS---
?!
WHAT
ARE YOU
DOING
WAY OUT
HERE?!

EX-CUSE
ME?!
"WHAT
ARE WE
DOING!?"
HE
MUST HAVE
THOUGHT
TWICE ABOUT
ATTACKING
THE BASE...

WE HEARD THAT YOU WERE GONNA TAKE ON THE RED RIBBON ARMY BY YOURSELF, SO WE CAME TO HELP!
THAT'S AMAZING! HOW DID YOU KNOW I WAS GONNA ATTACK THEM?!
BECAUSE WE KNOW HOW STUPID YOU ARE?

IN ANY CASE, YOU WERE WISE NOT TO GO THROUGH WITH IT!
HUH ?

I'M NOT WISE! I *DID* ATTACK 'EM!
WHAT ?!

YEAH! AND I BEAT EVERYBODY UP AND NOW I HAVE 6 DRAGON BALLS!

EEP?!

WH-WHEN YOU SAY YOU BEAT EVERYBODY UP... YOU DON'T MEAN THE WHOLE RED RIBBON ARMY...? NOT BY YOURSELF...?
SURE! EXCEPT THE ONES THAT RAN AWAY!

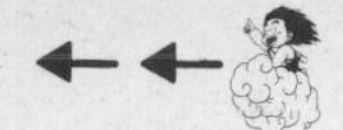

P-PU'AR, COULD YOU.... CHECK OUT THE BASE?
Y-YES SIR!

IT'S TRUE--!!
THE BASE HAS BEEN-- DECIMATED!!
I DON'T BELIEVE IT!

HE JUST KEEPS SURPRISING ME...
THE POLICE COULDN'T BEAT THEM...THE ARMY COULDN'T BEAT THEM...
BUT THAT LITTLE SQUIRT...
IT'S A MIRACLE...
NAW! I JUST GOT STRONGER AGAIN!

YOU CLIMBED IT A LONG TIME AGO, TOO, DIDN'T YOU, OLD TIMER? THAT BIG POLE?
WHAT?!
Y-YOU CLIMBED IT?! THE K-KARIN TOWER?
?
YUP! AND I MET MASTER KARIN, TOO!
AND I EVEN GOT TO DRINK THE MAGIC WATER!!

Y-YES... THAT IS HOW I GAINED SOME OF MY OWN GREAT STRENGTH....
NO POINT MENTIONING THAT IT TOOK ME 3 YEARS TO GET THE WATER...

WHAT ARE YOU TALKING ABOUT?!
BULMA!! THAT'S RIGHT!!

THE DRAGON RADAR BROKE AGAIN! COULD YOU FIX IT?
WHAT?! YOU'VE GATHERED SIX OF THE SEVEN BUT YOU STILL HAVEN'T FOUND YOUR GRAND-FATHER'S HEIRLOOM BALL?!

YEAH, I DID ACTUALLY, BUT... SEE...

I PROMISED THIS KID UPA WHOSE DAD GOT KILLED BY THOSE RED RIBBON GUYS THAT I'D ASK THE DRAGON GOD TO RESURRECT HIM, SO I NEED ALL SEVEN!

I SEE....
GOKU! YOU ARE TRULY HEROIC!

WELL, I CAN'T FIX IT HERE. LET'S HEAD BACK TO THE TURTLE HOUSE....
OK!

HYOOOON

THAT BOY JUST GETS STRONGER BY THE HOUR, DOESN'T HE?
HE'S QUITE A FELLOW, INDEED.

HE MAY EVEN BE STRONGER THAN ME AT THIS POINT...
WHAT--?! A-ARE YOU SERIOUS--?!

I'M NOT SURE, MIND YOU, BUT I HAVE MY DOUBTS AS TO WHETHER...
...EVEN I WOULD HAVE THE STAMINA TO TAKE DOWN THE ENTIRE RED RIBBON ARMY...

HO HO HO... HE IS AN INESTIMABLE LAD ALREADY... AND I SUSPECT HE HAS A LONG WAY TO GO YET!
WOW...

IF ONE OF US WERE THINKING OF ENTERING THE NEXT *TENKA'ICHI BUDÔKAI*, WE SHOULD KISS FIRST PLACE GOODBYE, HM?
OH, YES.
D'OH!

AND TO THINK THAT UNTIL JUST RECENTLY, WE WERE ALMOST EQUAL IN ABILITY...

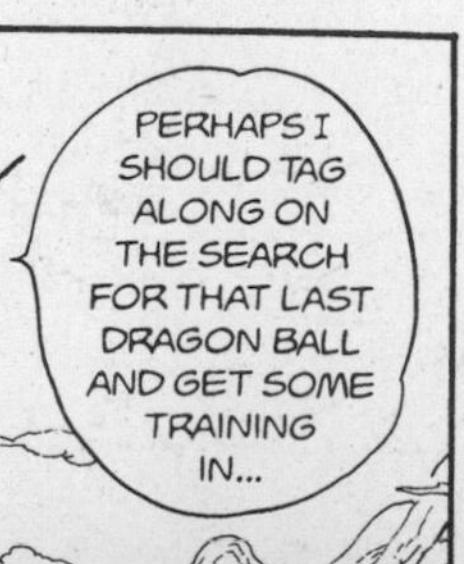
PERHAPS I SHOULD TAG ALONG ON THE SEARCH FOR THAT LAST DRAGON BALL AND GET SOME TRAINING IN...

M-MAYBE I'LL GO TOO...

KAME HOUSE

THAT'S FUNNY...

NOTHING'S BROKEN...
BUT THE LAST ONE DOESN'T SHOW UP!

MAYBE IT FLEW INTO OUTER SPACE?
IT COULDN'T FLY THAT FAR.

ALL OF THEM *WERE* THERE UNTIL JUST LATELY.

...WHICH MEANS...
MAYBE SOMEONE OR SOMETHING SWALLOWED IT...!

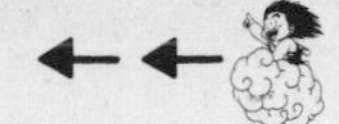

SWALLOWED?! A DRAGON BALL?!
WHY NOT?
THE DISTINCT RADIO WAVES EMITTED BY THE BALLS ARE BLOCKED BY BIOLOGICAL MATTER.

WHAT IDIOT WOULD SWALLOW SOMETHING LIKE THAT?!
AN ANIMAL COULD HAVE... AN ALLIGATOR... A HIPPO-POTAMUS...!

THEN... DOES THAT MEAN THERE'S NO WAY TO FIND IT?
I'M AFRAID SO! THERE'S NOTHING WE CAN DO!

B-BUT THAT'S NO GOOD...
WHAT SHOULD I DO...?

MAYBE IT'LL BE POOPED OUT!
COULD YOU HAVE PUT THAT MORE DELICATELY?!
COULD EVEN A HIPPO POOP THAT THING OUT?

DANG...
...AND ALL I'VE GOTTA DO IS FIND THAT ONE...

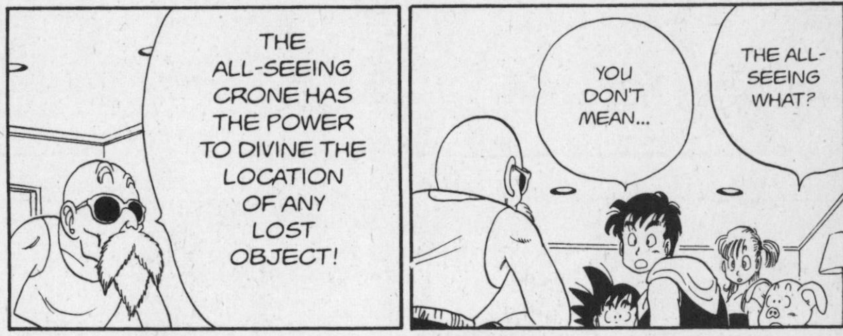

* "URANAI" MEANING "FORTUNETELLER" AND "BABA" MEANING "CRONE"—ED.

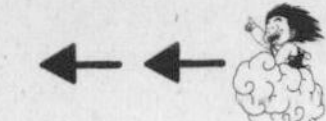

NEXT: The Palace of Mystery

WHO IS THIS "ALL-SEEING CRONE" KAME-SEN'NIN SAYS CAN FIND ANY SOUGHT OBJECT? AND HOW IS GOKU'S STRENGTH NEEDED TO WIN HER HELP? KNOWING KAME-SEN'NIN, THERE'S A LOT TO THIS STORY THAT HASN'T BEEN TOLD.....

Tale 98 • The All-Seeing Crone

SURPLUS
BOB'S
SALOON

NO WAY----!
I AM NOT WEARIN' ANYTHING LIKE *THIS*--!

HA-HAHA-HAHA!!!
MAYBE THE CRONE WILL FEEL SORRY FOR YOU!

HOW DO YOU LIKE IT?
I WANT TO WEAR WHAT I ALWAYS DO!

THEN WHY DON'T I RECREATE THE SAME PATTERN FOR YOU?
IF YOU CAN DO IT QUICKLY.
YAY!

AND WOULD YOU LIKE ME TO INCLUDE THIS "TURTLE-IN-A-CIRCLE" MARK?

YUP! AND PUT IT WHERE IT'S TORN OUT IN THE FRONT, TOO! AND DON'T FORGET A HOLE FOR MY TAIL!

WELL, IT'S A SIMPLE PATTERN, SO...
IT SHOULDN'T TAKE ME MORE THAN AN HOUR.
JUST BE SURE TO USE YOUR CHEAPEST FABRIC.

WHAT SHOULD WE DO?
WE COULD KILL SOME TIME IN THE SALOON.
WHAT-EVER.
I'LL GO GET UPA WHILE WE WAIT!

HE'LL BE SO HAPPY TO HEAR HOW CLOSE WE ARE TO GETTING ALL THE DRAGON BALLS TOGETHER!

WELL, ALL RIGHT-- JUST MAKE SURE YOU DON'T GET LOST!!
NO CHANCE !!
HYUUUN
SHERIFF

THERE IT IS, THERE IT IS!!

TOP

UPA!! ARE YOU THERE-- IT'S ME, GOKU--!!

GOKU ?...

OH--!!! IT *IS* YOU-- GOKU!!

YOU'RE ALIVE!! I'M SO GLAD !!
WHY WOULDN'T I BE?
I'VE BEEN PRAYING FOR YOU THE *WHOLE* TIME!
YOU'RE FUNNY! ANYWAY, I BEAT UP THOSE RED GUYS--
AND I'VE GOT SIX DRAGON BALLS TOGETHER NOW! ONE MORE AND WE CAN BRING YOUR DAD BACK TO LIFE! SO COME ON!

WHERE'S THE SEVENTH BALL?!
WE DON'T KNOW YET, BUT THERE'S SOMEBODY WHO'S GONNA TELL US!

UM... TH-THIS IS THE FIRST TIME I'VE BEEN OUT-SIDE KARIN...
I'M A LITTLE SCARED...
DON'T WORRY! I WAS LIKE THAT TOO, BUT THERE'S SO MUCH OUT THERE THAT'S SO FUN!
DO YOU THINK I CAN EVER BE STRONG LIKE YOU, GOKU?
OF COURSE! WHEN YOUR DAD'S ALIVE AGAIN, HAVE HIM TRAIN YOU!

THIS IS UPA!
N-NICE TO MEET YOU.
H-HI... HEH HEH
I'M PU'AR.
GOKU, YOUR CLOTHES ARE READY.

SHE'S PRETTY CUTE...

YOU'RE A BOY, RIGHT ?
YES !

O-OH... RIGHT...I KNEW THAT...
FEH
I'M FINALLY FIGURING OUT HOW TO TELL A BOY FROM A GIRL JUST BY LOOKING!
WOULD YOU DO THAT IN PRIVATE, PLEASE... ?!
OHO HO HO!
WHISKY

AND STOP SCRATCH-ING YOURSELF !!!
SKRITCH SKRATCH

HEH HEH--
NEW SHOES, TOO !!
THANKS, YAMCHA !

PU'AR, ABOUT HOW MUCH LONGER?
IT SHOULD BE SOMEWHERE AROUND HERE...

"SOMEWHERE AROUND HERE" IS NOTHING BUT DESERT...
BUT ACCORDING TO THE MAP LORD MUTEN-RÔSHI GAVE US, IT SHOULD BE...
HEY! THERE'S A BUILDING BY THAT LAKE OVER THERE!

INDEED!! THAT MUST BE IT!!

HYUUNNN

THIS PLACE IS AWFULLY HOT, ISN'T IT....?
LOOKS LIKE THERE ARE SOME OTHER PEOPLE HERE ALREADY....
CAPSULE CORP.

EXCUSE ME....
GLARE

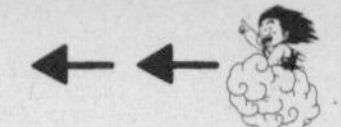

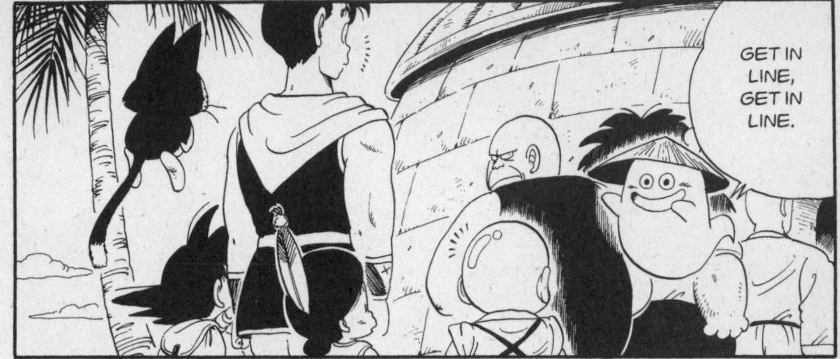

GET IN LINE, GET IN LINE.

HEY, IS THIS THE BALL-SEEING CRONE'S HOUSE?
THAT'S THE ALL-SEEING CRONE, BOY!

ARE THE FIVE OF YOU TOGETHER?
UHHH... Y-YES, WE ARE... BUT....

HEH HEH HEH--
INDEED--?
I SEE....

WELL THEN... I SHALL CALL YOU WHEN YOUR TURN ARRIVES....
WEIRDO.

WHY DO YOU SUPPOSE...
EVERYONE IN FRONT LOOKS SO.... TOUGH...?

OH, WHAT ARE YOU WORRYIN' ABOUT?! THEY'RE PROBABLY JUST A BUNCH OF BUDDIES FROM A MARTIAL ARTS SCHOOL!

MY MY-- SO THAT WAS IT, REALLY!
NOW THAT YOU MENTION IT, I *DID* LEAVE IT THERE! MY SOLID GOLD PICKLING STONE!
HOW WONDERFUL, MY DEAR!

SEE? THEY'RE NOT ALL TOUGH GUYS!
YEAH...
HYUUUUN

WILL THE NEXT GROUP PLEASE FOLLOW ME--?
YEAH!!! GO!!! LET'S GET 'EM!

...TH-THEY SURE ARE... FULL OF *OOMPH*, THOUGH, AREN'T THEY...?
...
IT *DOES* SEEM A BIT ODD...

AAAGH!! NO!! MERCY!!!
D-DO YOU GUYS HEAR WHAT I'M HEARIN'... ?
WH-WHAT'S GOING ON?

BETTER LUCK NEXT TIME!
SORRY, FOLKS...
WHINE
WHINE WHINE
GAK !!

HEH HEH HEH HEH--
WH-WHAT HAPPENED TO THOSE FELLOWS ?
WH-WHAT THE-- ?!
THANKS FOR WAITING...

COME THIS WAY, PLEASE.....
...

RIGHT THROUGH HERE.
L-LORD YAMCHA--?
I CAN'T EXACTLY BLAME YOU...
I-I'M SCARED...

ARE'NT YOU ALL SO ***YOUNG***?
MY MY!

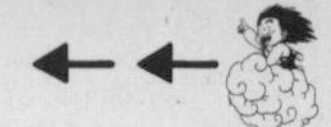

ARE YOU THE ALL-SEEING BONE?
THAT'S ALL-SEEING CRONE !!!

WHAT A WEIRD NAME.
IT'S NOT MY NAME! IT'S MY PROFESSIONAL TITLE !!

OH. OKAY.
THERE'S SOMETHING I WANT YOU TO FIND FOR ME.

VERY WELL.
THAT WILL BE 10 MILLION ZENI.

T-TEN MILLION ZENI--- ?!
W-WE NEED MONEY ?!!

HOW WOULD WE EVER GET THAT MUCH MONEY ?!
NOT ENOUGH TO PAY, EH?

IN THAT CASE, COME THIS WAY.
WH-WHAT ARE YOU GOING TO DO...?

***NEXT:* The Five Champions**

SO BASICALLY WHAT YOU'RE SAYING IS THAT IF WE FIGHT ONE BY ONE AND WE DEFEAT FIVE OF YOUR CHAMPIONS, YOU'LL DO YOUR MYSTICAL DIVINATION FOR FREE?

INDEED...BUT YOU ALL ARE MERE CHILDREN. IT'S AN IMPOSSIBLE DREAM.

Tale 99 • The Five Champions

HEH HEH HEH. I FEEL SORRY FOR THESE CHAMPIONS OF YOURS.
WHAT ARE THE RULES?
NOT MANY. IF YOU BEG FOR MERCY OR FALL IN THE LAKE, YOU LOSE.

AND WITH THAT, LET US BEGIN.
WHO WILL START FOR YOUR SIDE ?

I WILL !!!
TMM

GOOD LUCK, KURIRIN !
HOPE YOU DON'T MIND NOT GETTING A TURN, GOKU! I MIGHT BEAT ALL FIVE BY MYSELF!

WOW...I'M HAVING FLASHBACKS OF THE STRONGEST-UNDER-THE-HEAVENS MARTIAL ARTS TOURNA-MENT...
COUNT DRACULA... ENTER !

FWAP FWAP

WHAT THE--? THAT'S A BAT!

I'M SUPPOSED TO FIGHT ***THIS***?

POOF

SKREEE !

TRA-LALALA
HEY! HE TURNED INTO A PERSON!
BUT A WEIRD PERSON...!
A KICK-BOXER...!
HEH HEH HEH...

SKREE SKREE SKREE!
FOOEY!
HE AIN'T GOT MUCH!

NOW, THEN!! LET THE MATCH BEGIN!!!

I'LL START LIGHT AND CHECK HIM OUT.

HYAH!!
FSH

POOF

HYOH
!
HUH
?!

OH
!
SKREEEEE
!

H-HE TURNED BACK INTO A BAT!!
HE'S QUICK, TOO
!

WHSH WHSH WHSH
NNN
NNNH
!!

VNNN
SHOOT-- !!
HE'S *TOO* QUICK !!
VNNN

POP
WAAH !!!

GLOMP
WAK !!!

OH !!

SLURP
SLURP
WAAH--!!!

HE'S A VAMPIRE !!!
HE'S SUCKING KURIRIN'S BLOOD !!!

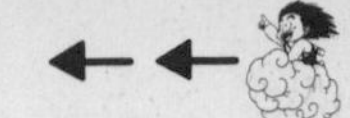

YAARGH--!!!
ST-STOP IT, YOU MONSTER--!!
KURIRIN, SHAKE HIM OFF--!!
HEE HEE HEE... SURRENDER SOON, OR YOU'LL PERISH FROM BLOOD LOSS!
FLAIL FLAIL

EE-YAAH--!!!
VSH

TAKE THIS!!!

SHP
GONG

HEH HEH HEH
ARE YOU ALL RIGHT, KURIRIN?!
OWWW... !!!

WOBBLE WOBBLE
YEEESH-- !!

NOW THAT'S A LAD WITH EXCELLENT TASTE!
"TASTE"! GET IT?!
BELCH

SPYEW
ACK !

MRRRR
Y-YOU DON'T KNOW ME, DO YOU...?!!

WELL, DO YOU GIVE UP?
SAY "MERCY" AND WE'LL GIVE YOU A TRANS-FUSION.

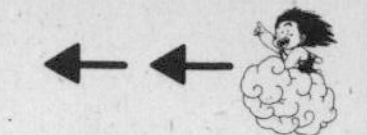

DON'T LOSE IT!! CENTER YOURSELF!!
IF YOU GET WORKED UP YOU BLEED MORE!!
NAMU-AMIDA-BUTSU...OM MANI PADME HUM...
EXHALE... EXHALE...

...PHEW...

HA HA HA!! HEY, KURIRIN, IT LOOKS LIKE YOU GREW HAIR!!
SNK
SHUT UP !!!
GUSSSH

WOBBLE WOBBLE WOBBLE WOBBLE
WHOA
WAAA

HEY !!!
GONG

SBLOTCH

OH!

SMIRK

HUDDLE HUDDLE
WHISPER WHISPER

UH... SORRY ABOUT THIS...
BUT WOULD IT BE ALL RIGHT FOR ALL 5 OF US TO FIGHT, AFTER ALL?!
I TOLD YOU SO! THAT'S WHAT YOU GET FOR BEING SO BOASTFUL.

HEY! SINCE THESE TWO ARE SO SHORT, CAN THEY FIGHT TOGETHER AS A TEAM?
WELL?
SKREE, SKREE, SKREE! I MEAN... OF COURSE!! WHAT A *TASTY* IDEA!!

I WILL ALLOW IT!
THANKS--!
ALL RIGHT... JUST FOLLOW THE PLAN, UNDER-STOOD?
MNCH MNCH
B-BUMP B-BUMP

NOW THEN...
LET THE MATCH BEGIN!!

GOOD LUCK, PU'AR!! UPA!!
SKREE SKREE SKREE SKREE!!

YIPPEE! YIPPEE!!
H-HERE HE COMES!!
FSSSH

PHYEW

GYAAA-UGGHH !!

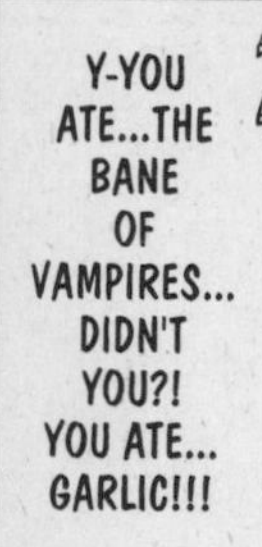
Y-YOU ATE...THE BANE OF VAMPIRES... DIDN'T YOU?! YOU ATE... GARLIC!!!

YURRRG-- !!
POOF
WELL THEN...I SHALL DRINK THE BLOOD OF YOUR COMPANION INSTEAD!!
PHYEW

SKREE SKREE-- !!

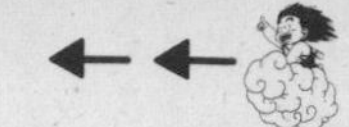

TRANS-
FORM...
INTO
A
PORCU-
PINE
!!!

BOM

CLOMP
!!

YEE-
OWWW--
!!!!

OWW..
OWW..

EH
?!

WH-WHAT
ARE
YOU
DOING...
?!
I AM THE
VAMPIRE'S
WORST
ENEMY...A
CRUCIFIX
!!

NEXT: The Mystery Challenger

THE POWERFUL "COUNT DRACULA," WHO DEFEATED KURIRIN, WAS BRILLIANTLY TAKEN DOWN BY THE STRATEGY OF PU'AR AND UPA! HOWEVER, THERE ARE STILL FOUR CHAMPIONS LEFT TO BATTLE....

Tale 100 • Battle of The Bleeders

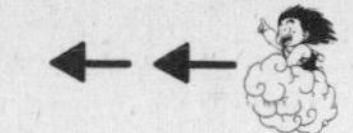

NO FAIR! I WANNA FIGHT TOO!
YOU'RE OUR EMERGENCY RESERVE. I'LL FIGHT FIRST.

NOW... BRING ON THE SECOND OPPONENT !
LORD YAMCHA, GOOD LUCK !!

HO HO HO...
HE'S ALREADY HERE.

EH ?!

WHERE? THERE'S NO ONE HERE!
VWIP
VWIP
WHAT'S THAT OLD CRONE TALKING ABOUT...

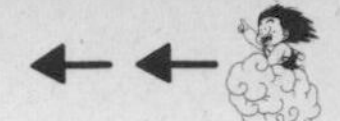

CAN'T SEE HIM, EH?! HEH HEH HEH!
OF COURSE NOT! HE'S THE INVISIBLE MAN!!

IN...
...VISIBLE MAN ?!

LET THE MATCH BEGIN !!!

HO HO HO, HERE I COME... !
GLLP

DMM
OOF !!!
BWAK

TH-THIS IS NOT FAIR...!
L-LORD YAMCHA-- !!

B-BAM B-BAM

DM DM DM DM
ARGH !!

WHERE ARE YOU...?!
SHOW YOURSELF, COWARD!!

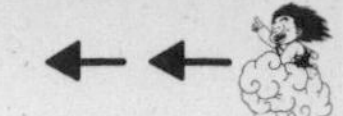

FEH !!!
VNNN

VSH
VSH
BLAST IT!!

PANT PANT
C-CURSE YOU... !!
HEH HEH HEH HEH... WHAT HAPPENED TO ALL THAT BRAVADO YOU WERE SHOWING JUST A MINUTE GO?

...
HEY!! WHAT'S YAMCHA DOING FIGHTING ALL BY HIMSELF?!

GOKU!! GO BRING THE INVINCIBLE OLD MASTER AND BULMA... QUICKLY!!
HUH? WHY?

IT DOESN'T MATTER WHY! JUST HURRY!!
OK...

VYOOOOON

UNGH
!!!
BWAK

A KINTO'UN... ?
WHO IN THE WORLD IS HE... ?

ALL I CAN DO IS TO TRY TO FIGURE OUT HIS POSITION FROM THE FAINT AIR MOVEMENTS CREATED EVERY TIME HE MOVES...

OHHH... !!!
AARGH!! AT THIS RATE, I DON'T HAVE A CHANCE!!

SHHP

SNEEEK

YOU'RE OVER HERE !!!
FWAA

CHK

TPP

WAHAHA! I TOUCHED YOU!
EVEN AN INVISIBLE MAN CAN'T CONCEAL HIMSELF COMPLETELY WHEN HE MOVES!

OH, YOU THINK NOT? *HEH HEH HEH....*

OH, THEY CALL ME THE ALL-SEEING CRRRRR-O-O-ONE!

IF THERE'S SOMETHING THAT YOU WOULD LIKE KNO-O-O-O-OWN---
ULP ?!

BWACH
!!

GLOM
B-KAM
THOG

K-
KEEP FIGHTING, LORD YAMCHA... !!

TEE HEE HEE!
HUFF
HUFF
I-IT'S NO GOOD...THAT HORRIBLE SINGING IS DROWNING OUT HIS MOVEMENTS... !!

DO YOU SURRENDER ?!
YOU DON'T HAVE A CHANCE, YOU KNOW, FORGIVE MY SAYING IT.

BLAST IT... IF I COULD ONLY **SEE** MY OPPONENT... !!

HEY, KURIRIN! I BROUGHT THEM-- !!
YES! AND WE STILL HAVE TIME!

OH MY...

WHAT IS THIS?! I WAS JUST ABOUT TO HEAD HOME!!
YOU HAD SOME-THING TO ASK US?

NOT REALLY...
I JUST WANTED YOU GUYS TO WATCH THIS MATCH FOR A LITTLE WHILE, THAT'S ALL.

"MATCH" ?!
BULMA, IF YOU'D PLEASE WATCH FROM OVER HERE.
LORD MUTEN-RÔSHI, PLEASE STAND OVER THERE!

OH!! WHAT ARE YOU DOING, YAMCHA?!
HURRY, OVER HERE, BULMA!
D-BOP D-BOP
YOW!! YOW!!

LORD MUTEN-RÔSHI, PLEASE FACE UPWARD JUST A LITTLE MORE!!
HUH?
WHAT THE--?! I CAN'T SEE ANYTHING LIKE THIS!
?
?

THIS IS A VERY TIRING POSITION TO WATCH FROM, YOU KNOW...
ARE YOU READY?!! HOLD IT RIGHT THERE, HOLD IT...

THIS IS IT!!!

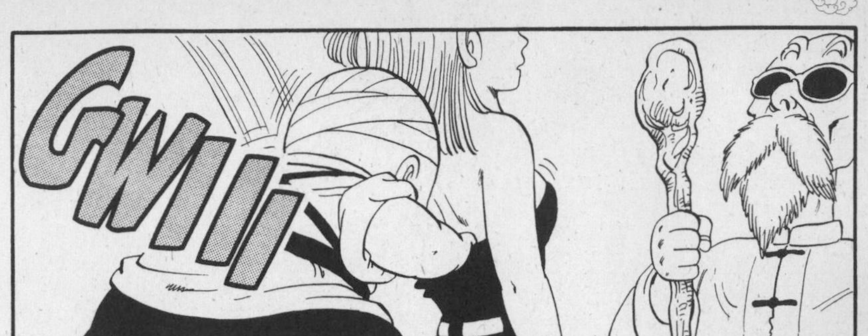
GWIII

BOINNG
!!

GUSSSH

WAAH !!!!
WHAT ?!
PLASSSH
HUH ?!

YES-- I CAN SEE HIM NOW !!!

OH !!!
WHOOPS !!!

FIST OF THE
WOLF-FANG GALE !

OH NO !!!

B-DAP-B-DAP

NEXT: The Haunt of Fear!

Tale 101 • The Devil's Cesspool

DID YOU JUST CALL HER....?
IMAGINE GROWING UP WITH HER!

WH-WHAT ?!

SNORT LONG TIME NO SEE.
NOT THAT YOU'VE CHANGED ONE IOTA.

STILL CAN'T CONTROL THOSE "NOSE-BLEEDS" OF YOURS, EH?
OH, STUFF IT.

B-BUT LORD MUTEN-RÔSHI...IF SHE'S YOUR SISTER...COULDN'T YOU PLEASE ASK HER TO DIVINE THE ANSWER FOR YOUR SAKE?

FORGET IT.
I LIVE FOR TWO THINGS. MONEY AND FIGHTS.

I DON'T MIND.
THIS WILL BE GOOD TRAINING, EH?

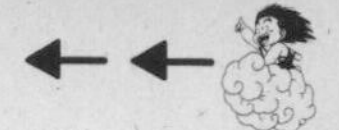

BOLDLY SAID. NOW, FOR THE NEXT OPPONENTS, WE'RE GOING TO CHANGE ARENAS.
FOLLOW ME.
SINCE WE'RE HERE ALREADY, WE MIGHT AS WELL JUST STAY AND WATCH...

HOW MUCH MONEY DO YOU HAVE, SIS?
YOU'LL NEVER KNOW, FREE-LOADER!

WHO ARE YOU?
OH, I'M UPA.

AHA! YOU'RE THE ONE WHOSE FATHER GOKU WANTS TO REVIVE WITH THE DRAGON BALLS, RIGHT?
YES!

YOU PROBABLY SHOULDN'T BE TALKING TO HER, UPA. SHE'S A BAD INFLUENCE.
LOOK WHO'S TALKING !!!

THIS WAY.
...

WHERE ON EARTH IS THIS MATCH GOING TO BE...?
THE DEVIL'S CESS-POOL.

TH-THE D-DEVIL'S CESSPOOL ?!

WH-WHAT KIND OF ARENA IS THIS ?!
DON'T YOU HAVE ANY ADVICE ?!
I DO !
DON'T DIE !
TAKE IT FROM ME.
...
THAT'S QUITE HELPFUL...

THE CONTESTANT ENTERS THROUGH HERE.
IF I MUST....

THE REST OF YOU COME THIS WAY. THERE'S AN EXCELLENT VIEW OF THE MATCH FROM UP HERE.

WH- WHAT THE-- ?!!!

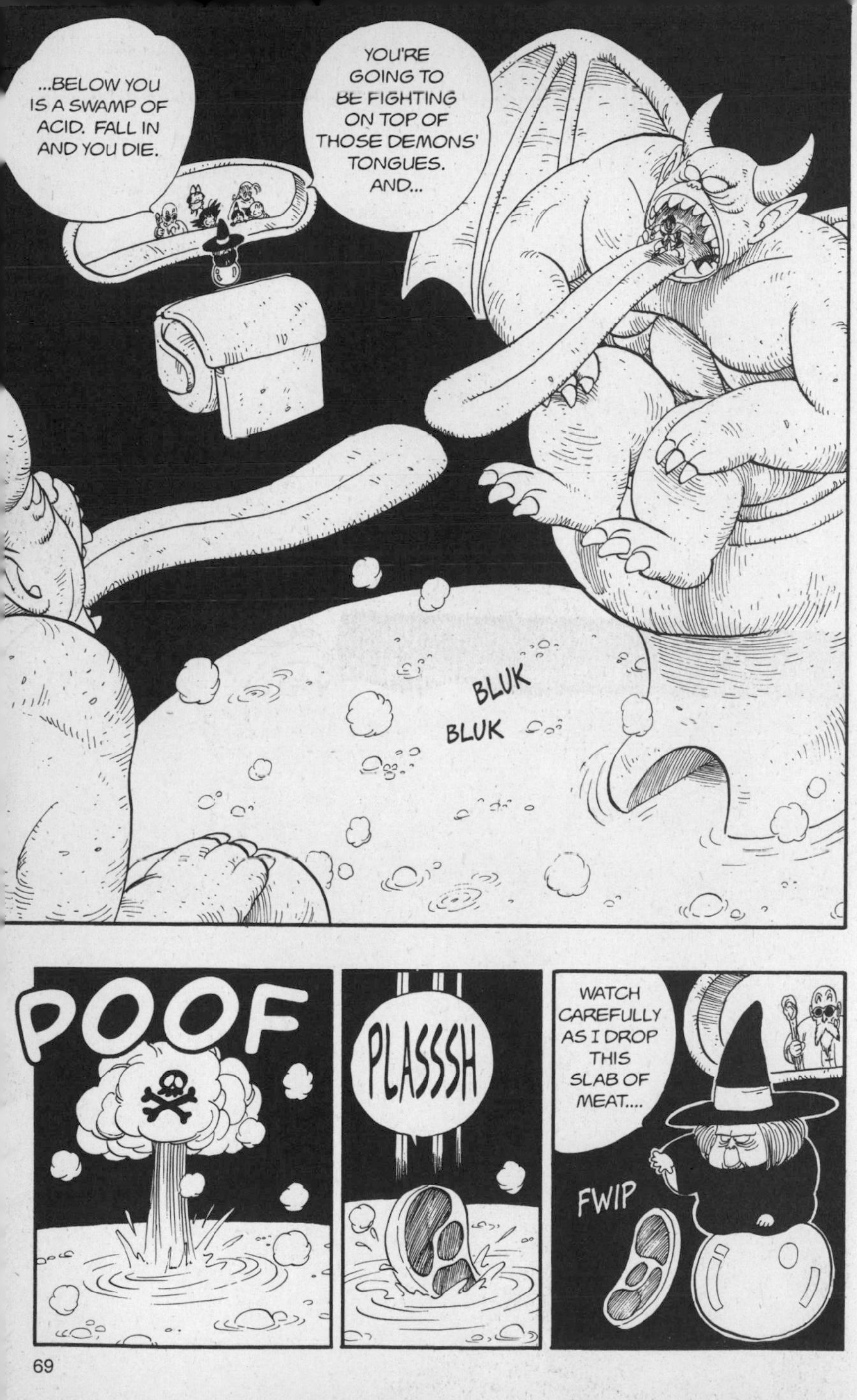

YOU'RE GOING TO BE FIGHTING ON TOP OF THOSE DEMONS' TONGUES. AND...

...BELOW YOU IS A SWAMP OF ACID. FALL IN AND YOU DIE.

BLUK
BLUK

AS YOU CAN SEE, ONE MISSTEP AND YOU'LL DISSOLVE COMPLETELY INTO NOTHINGNESS.
OOOO... !!!

ACK... !!

IF YOU WANT TO CALL OFF THE MATCH, NOW'S THE TIME.
YOU STILL HAVE SO MUCH TO LIVE FOR.

I-I SEE...
THE DEVIL'S CESSPOOL, INDEED... !

I L-LIVE FOR BATTLE !

HEE HEE HEE! NOW THAT'S THE SPIRIT!

WELL THEN, LET ME INTRODUCE YOU TO MY THIRD CHAMPION...

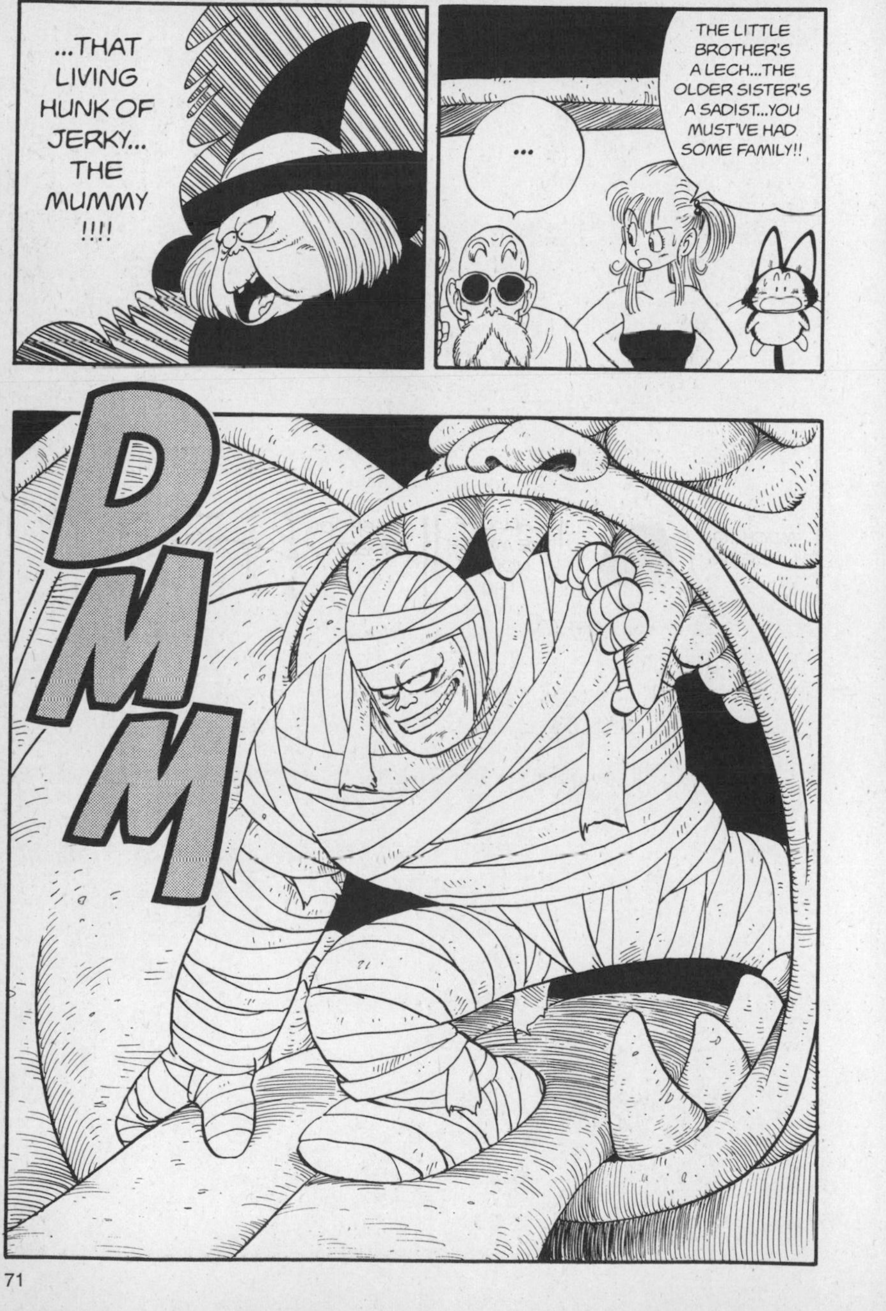

THE LITTLE BROTHER'S A LECH...THE OLDER SISTER'S A SADIST...YOU MUST'VE HAD SOME FAMILY!!
...

...THAT LIVING HUNK OF JERKY... THE MUMMY !!!!

DMM

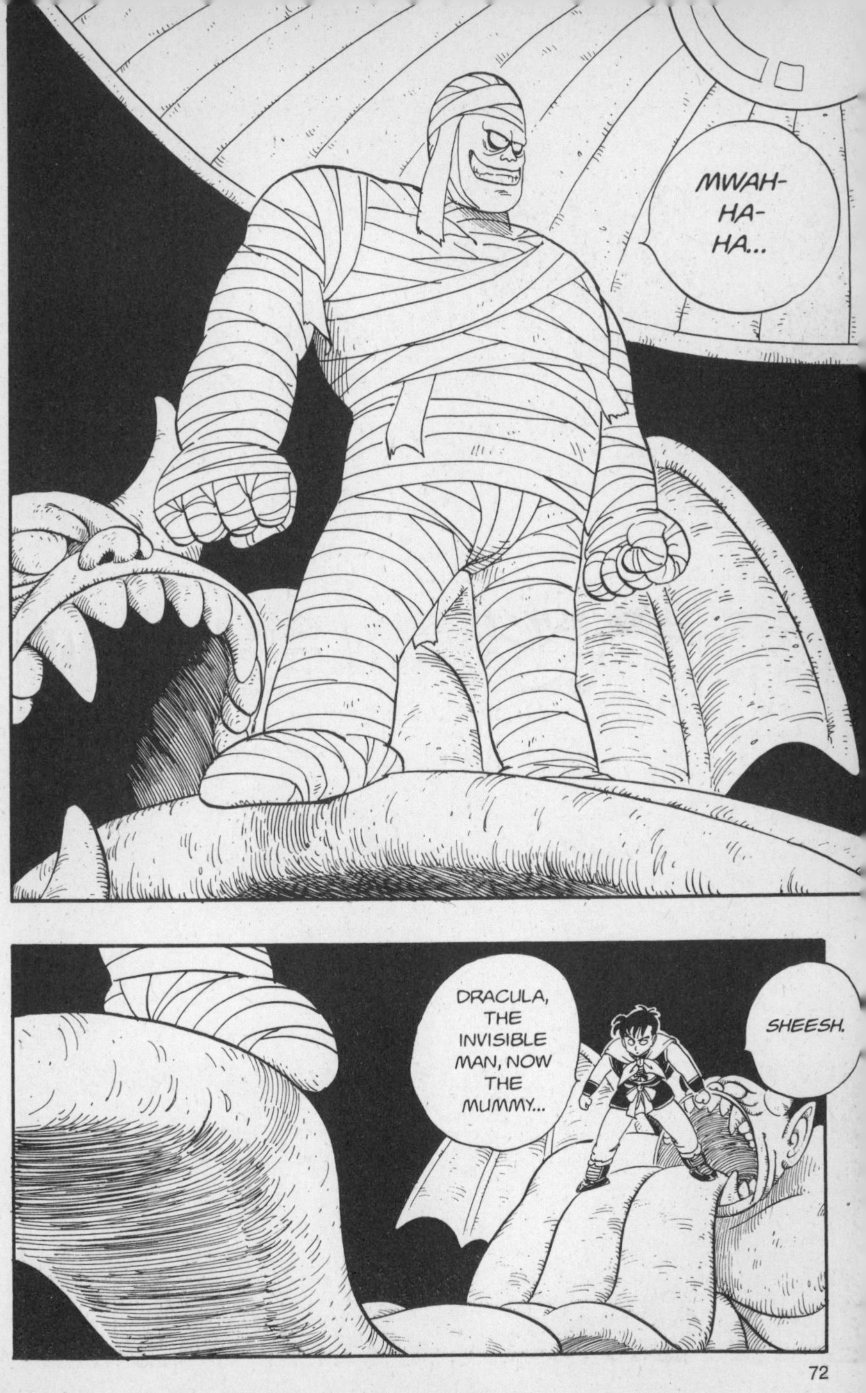

MWAH-HA-HA...

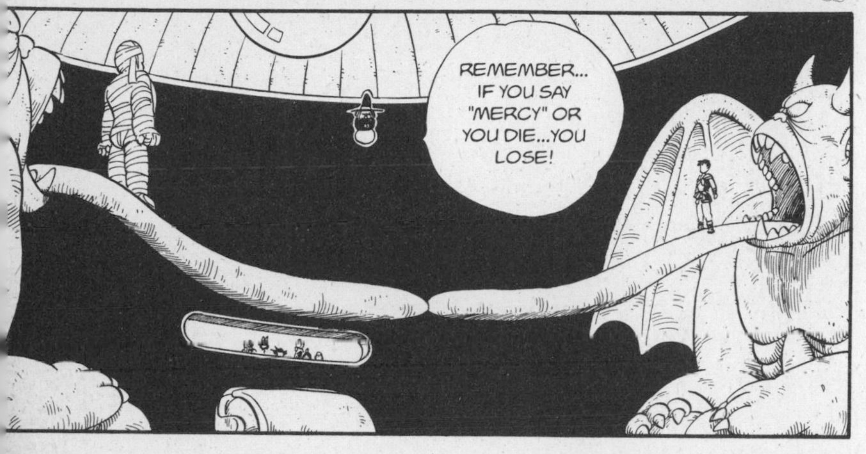

REMEMBER... IF YOU SAY "MERCY" OR YOU DIE...YOU LOSE!

NOW BEGIN !!!!

LOOKS LIKE THE TYPE WHO BOWLS OPPONENTS OVER BY SHEER STRENGTH...
ALL RIGHT, THEN! I'LL USE THIS NARROW WALKWAY TO *MY* ADVANTAGE AND FIGHT HIM WITH MY SPEED AND MOVES!

LORD YAMCHA, PLEASE BE CAREFUL-- !!

TSUOH--
!!!
VSH
DOM

WHA
?!

TNG

STUP
VNNN
AIEE !!!
FNN FSH
VSH
BAPPITA BAPPITA

KLOK

NEXT: Goku at the Plate!

Tale 102 • Goku at the Plate!

QUIT WASTING TIME!! JUST BEAT THE GAUZE OFF THAT STIFF!!
YOU CAN DO IT, LORD YAMCHA-- !!

NOW FACE-- THE FIST OF THE WOLF FANG GALE !!!

VSSH

VSSH

HYAH--
!!!!
JAB JAB JAB

FPP
WAAH
!!!

VSSH

DOOOM

G-
GUGG

LORD YAMCHA--!!!

I'M GETTING BORED. WHY DON'T YOU JUST SURRENDER?
NNGH...!

HEE
HEE
HEE...
I DON'T
THINK HE
CAN HEAR
YOU!

RRR-
RRH
!!!
FSSSH

!!

H-HE'S
FALLING!!!
YAMCHA
DID IT
!!!

FORGIVE ME...!
SSHHF

EH--
?!
KWRRR
HYOOON
GNG
VOOM

FSSHH

STUP

WHOA
!!!!

SNEER

FEH! YOU'LL STOOP TO ANY TRICK, WON'T YOU?
WELL, I HOPE YOU'RE PREPARED TO PAY FOR IT.

AUGH !!!
SSS

HYOOO

TMMM

WOOP

GLONG

DO YOU SURRENDER?
OR WOULD YOU RATHER BE HURLED INTO THE ACID?!

A DULL FIGHT...BUT MERCIFULLY SHORT!
HEH HEH HEH

I... I SURRENDER....
HA! YOU SHOULD HAVE SAID THAT A LONG TIME AGO!

GAG HAK
LORD YAMCHA--!!!
YAMCHA-- ARE YOU ALL RIGHT?!

HMM...I THINK WE NEED TO REEVALUATE WHAT WE'RE UP AGAINST HERE...
I'M...S-SORRY, GOKU... I DIDN'T EXPECT...HIM TO BE SO TOUGH....

THAT WAS PATHETIC! I MEAN, LOOK AT THAT GUY! HE'S IN BANDAGES!
UH...I DON'T THINK HE'S IN BANDAGES CUZ HE'S HURT...

HEE HEE HEE... NOW, WHO'S THE LAST OF YOUR FIVE CHAMPIONS? IT'S YOUR TURN....
OR WOULD YOU RATHER JUST GIVE UP RIGHT NOW?
THAT'S ME!! AN' I'M READY TO FIGHT!!

G-GOKU-- PLEASE!! YOU'VE DONE ENOUGH!! YOU DON'T HAVE TO DO THIS!!
DON'T WORRY! LEAVE IT TO ME!!

JUST DON'T GET KILLED, GOKU!!
NO WAY !!

HMP.

HO.

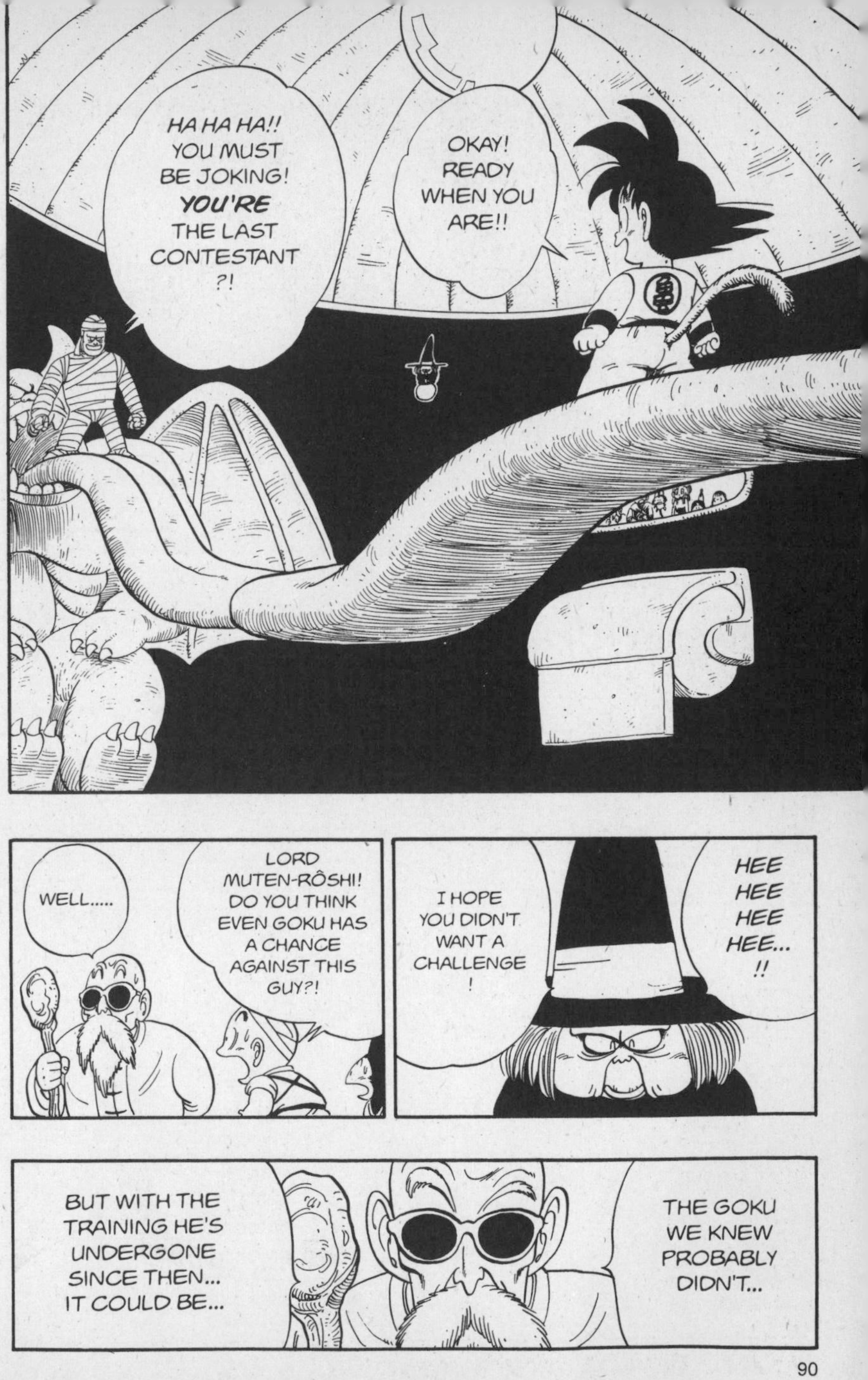

OKAY! READY WHEN YOU ARE!!
HA HA HA!! YOU MUST BE JOKING! ***YOU'RE*** THE LAST CONTESTANT ?!

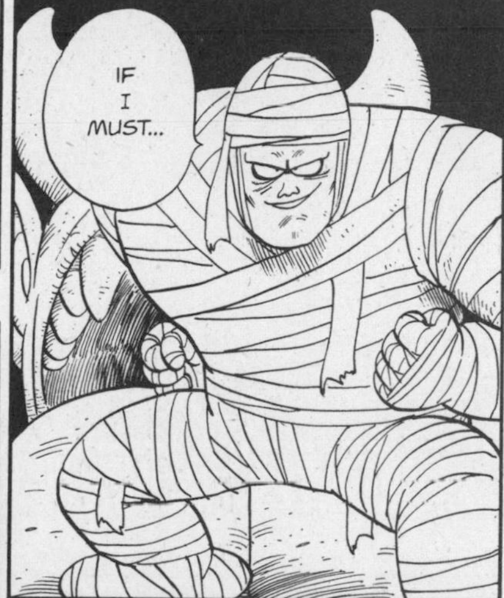

NEXT: Crying for Mummy

Tale 103 • The Power of Goku

ALL RIGHT !!!!

YOU ASKED FOR IT !!!!

OH
NO!!!
HE TOOK
IT FULL
FORCE
!!!

HYAH
!!!!

BWOK

KRAK
GWAM
!!

DOMP

...OH...

HEH! THAT WAS EASY!
WHAT WAS I WORRYING ABOUT, ANYWAY?!

HEH HEH HEH... LOSING CONSCIOUSNESS COUNTS AS A LOSS, OF COURSE.
BOY! IF YOU'RE STILL CONSCIOUS, SAY SOMETHING!
WELL? SPEAK!

OKAY !!

TWIK

WHAT-- ?!

NOW IT'S MY TURN !!!
VSH VSH
ARE YOU READY ?!

H-HE'S EVEN STRONGER THAN I THOUGHT....
TO TAKE AN ASSAULT LIKE THAT WITHOUT BLOCKING... WITHOUT BRUISES....

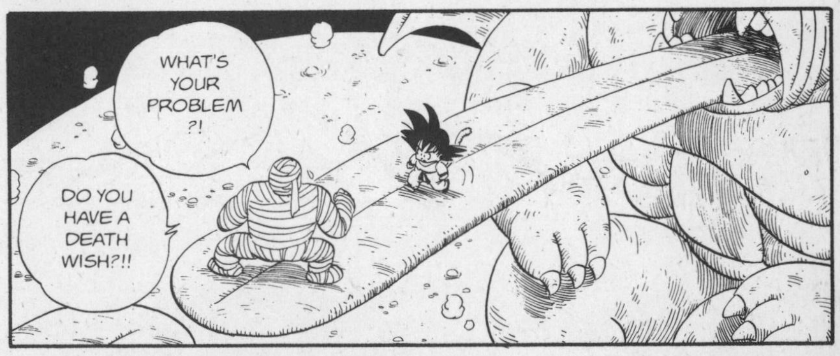
WHAT'S YOUR PROBLEM ?!
DO YOU HAVE A DEATH WISH?!!

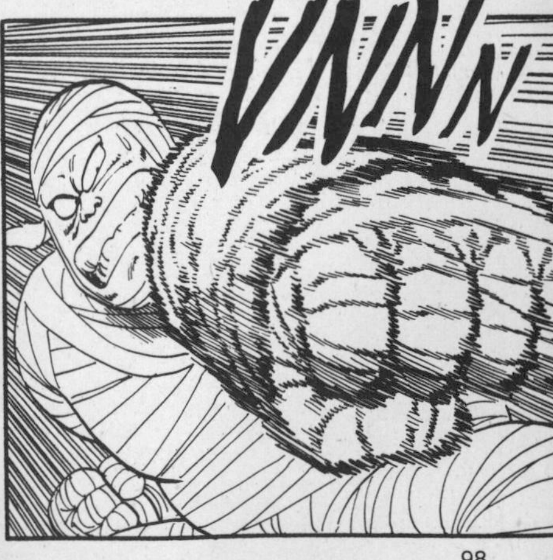
VNNN

FSH

DMM

!!

DOMP

HEY, ARE YOU AWAKE?
DOESN'T LOOK LIKE IT... THAT MEANS I WIN, RIGHT, CRONE ?

UH...
I... SUPPOSE SO....

HOO-HOO, I DID IT! I DID IT!
ZLURG ZLURG
HE'LL BE IN THE WAY IN THE NEXT FIGHT, SO I'LL MOVE HIM!

GASSSP

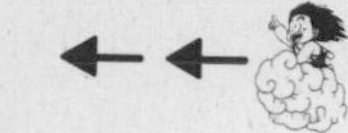

...A
S-S-SINGLE
BLOW...?
TH-THAT'S
IMPOSSIBLE...
WH-
WHAT'S
THIS
ABOUT...?

I DIDN'T THINK
EVEN HE COULD
HAVE BECOME *SO*
POWERFUL....
I'M NOT
SURE
WE'VE
SEEN THE
LIKE OF
THIS
BEFORE...

YOU
MEAN...
SON'S THAT
STRONG
?
I'M AS
SHOCKED AS
YOU ARE...
NO WONDER
HE WAS ABLE
TO DECIMATE
THE RED RIBBON
ARMY ALL BY
HIMSELF...

SHEESH...
I HAD NO IDEA...
HE DOESN'T
LOOK ANY
DIFFERENT...
WHAT'S HE
GONE THROUGH
SINCE WE
MET LAST...?

I ONLY
NEED
TO BEAT
TWO MORE
GUYS,
RIGHT
?!

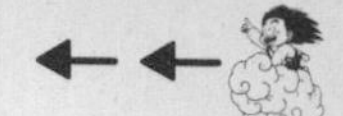

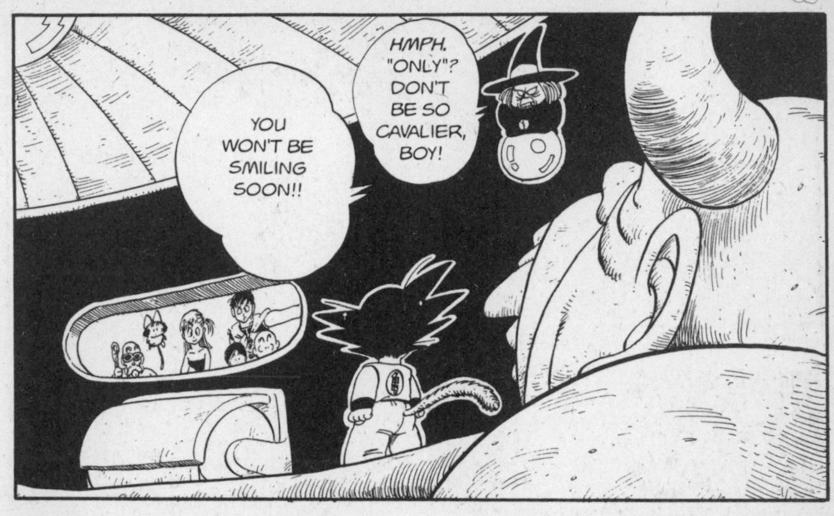

THAT BRAT HAS POWER...

HEH HEH HEH

WHAT'S SO FUNNY...?

OH, NOTHING. NOTHING AT ALL. *HEH.*

HE'S THE FIRST WHO'S EVER MADE IT THIS FAR...

BUT HIS LUCK RUNS OUT AGAINST ME!

ALL RIGHT--! THE 4TH CHAMPION !!
IT'S YOUR TURN-- **DEVIL** !!!

ARE YOU GUYS **ALL** WEIRDOS ?

WHAT?! SHE'S BRINGING THE DEVIL OUT ALREADY?! HE ALWAYS USED TO BE HER **RIGHT-HAND MAN!!** THAT MEANS...
SHE'S SAVING AN EVEN MORE INCREDIBLE FOE FOR LAST!!

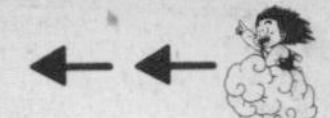

BEGIN
!

FWAP
FWAP
ACK!
FWAP

HEY, THAT'S NO FAIR!!
HE CAN FLY !!

CARE TO VISIT MY PLACE, BOY?! CARE TO VISIT...
...HELL ?!!

SHOOP

BON VOYAGE !!!!

HYAH !!!!

!!!

BOK

NEXT: Goku vs. The Devil

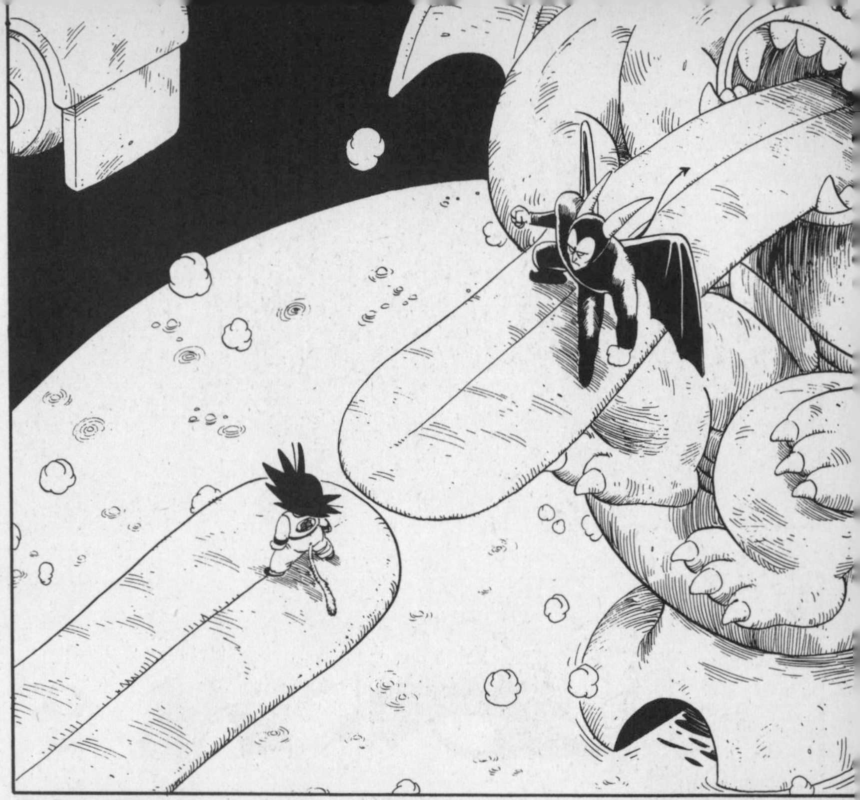

Tale 104 • The Beam of Evil

SPARE US THE TALKING, DEVIL!! JUST TAKE CARE OF HIM!!
Y-YES, MA'AM !!

HYOH !!!
BWONG
...

VNNn
OOPS.

FWAH
BOING

VNNN

AUGH !!

DONK
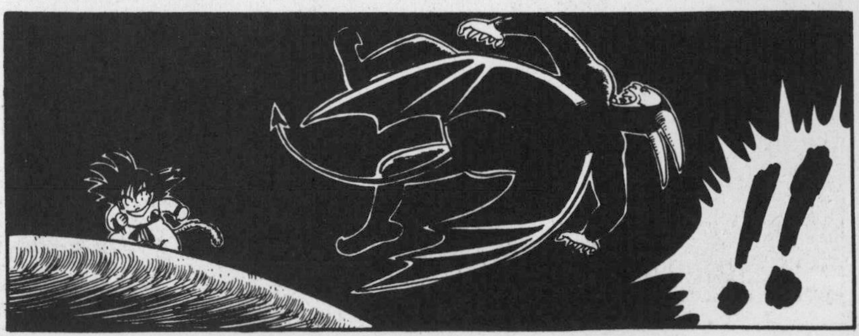
!!

HYOOOOOO

UNGH !!!
FWAP

FWAP
FWAP

PANT PANT
HEH HEH HEH HEH... Y-YOU THINK YOU CAN TAKE DOWN THE ***D-DEVIL*** WITH NO MORE THAN THAT, D-DO YOU... ?!

NAW! I WAS JUST TESTING YOU !
WH-WHAT ?!!

FOR A "DEVIL" HE DOESN'T SEEM LIKE MUCH!
IT ONLY LOOKS THAT WAY!

THE DEVIL IS A TWO-TIME CHAMPION OF THE STRONGEST-UNDER-THE-HEAVENS MARTIAL ARTS TOURNAMENT!
IT'S JUST THAT GOKU IS THAT MUCH BETTER!

WHOA....
A TWO-TIME CHAMPION.....?

DEVIL!!
CAN'T YOU DO ANY BETTER THAN THAT?!!!

OF C-COURSE I CAN, M'LADY.
NOW I'LL SHOW MY TRUE STRENGTH!

TNG
HUH?

EVEN THE MOST SWEET-FACED LITTLE GOODY-GOODY HAS A DROP OF EVIL IN HIS HEART.
I CAN MAKE THAT LITTLE DROP IN YOU EXPAND AND EXPAND AND EXPAND UNTIL...

YOU'RE BLOWN TO BITS !!!

?
HUH ?

NO !!
IT'S THE BEAM OF EVIL!! HE REALLY *IS* PLANNING TO KILL GOKU !!

HYOH!!!

DEVIL, WAIT-- !!

YOU DON'T HAVE TO GO THAT FAR... !!!

WHAT THE--?!

BOMM

FWA-HAHAHAHA! LET THE EVIL IN YOUR HEART GROW AND GROW!!!

EXPLODE
!!!!
WA-
HAHAHA-
HAHA--
!!!!

G-
GOKU
!!!
I-IT'S
TOO
LATE--
!!!

NOW
!!
BOOM
!!

BOOM...
BOO...

!!

HEY
!
WHAT WAS THAT ALL ABOUT?!

D-
DON'T.... DON'T TELL ME....
YOU DON'T HAVE ANY EVIL IN YOUR HEART AT ALL... ?!

POOF
IT DISAP-PEARED... ?

WHAT...WHAT IS THIS CHILD...?
HIS HEART IS LIKE A BABY'S...OR AN ANIMAL'S...!!

YEE-EAH !!
HE'S SAVED !!
PHEW
HMM... EITHER HIS THOUGHTS ARE UTTERLY PURE...OR HIS MIND WAS UTTERLY BLANK.... EITHER WAY, HE'S ALIVE.

GOSH. I WONDER HOW INNOCENT OLD ***YOU*** WOULD HAVE DONE WITH THAT BEAM.
YOU CAN'T JUST ENJOY A HAPPY ENDING, CAN YOU?
I MUST RESORT... TO MY ULTIMATE MOVE !
POP
OH !!

WAH !!
SHFF

THAT'S CHEATING!! USING A WEAPON!! FOOEY!!

HYOOO
AWP !!

OKAY, THEN!! IF THAT'S HOW YOU WANT IT, I'LL GET SERIOUS TOO!!

VNNN
D-GOOM
KRAK

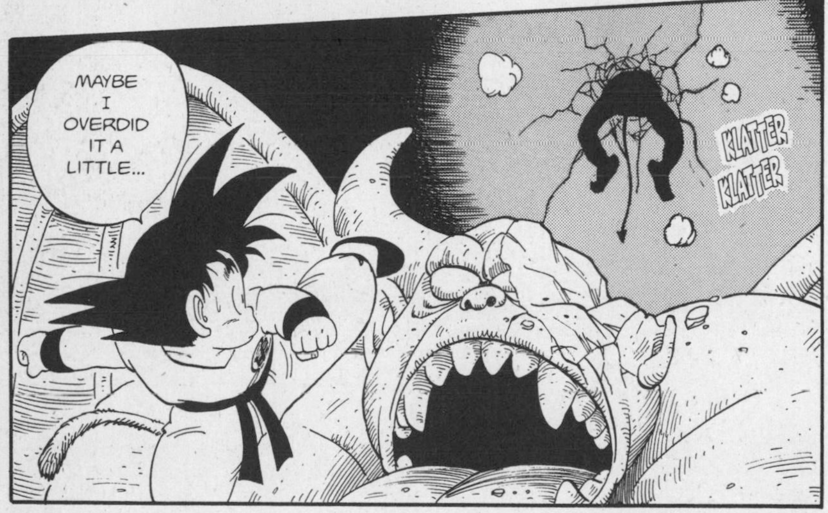

NEXT: The Last Champion!

Tale 105 • The Last Champion

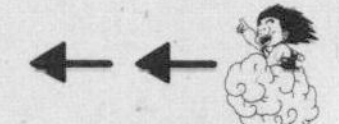

ONLY ONE MORE!! BRING 'IM ON!!!

HMPH! I HAVE TO ADMIT... YOU'RE THE FIRST GROUP TO HAVE PROGRESSED THIS FAR.
BUT YOU HAVE NEVER MET A WARRIOR... LIKE THE LAST CHAMPION! *HEE HEE HEE...*

NOW, THE TIME HAS COME !!!

THE TIME FOR...

ME !!

...HUH? ...
H-HI.

WHAT THE HECK?! TH-THAT'S THE ACE UP HER SLEEVE...?!

MADAME CRONE, I WAS WONDERING... WELL...
EH? WELL? WHAT IS IT?

I'D LIKE TO FIGHT THIS BOY ALL-OUT, NO HOLDS BARRED. SO...
I WAS WONDERING IF IT WOULD BE POSSIBLE TO LEAVE THIS LITTLE ROOM AND GO TO THE OUTSIDE ARENA... ?

HO... I SEE.
VERY WELL, WHY NOT?

BUT YOU'RE GOING TO WIN THIS, RIGHT?

WELL... I LIKE TO THINK SO....

CHEEZ! YOU GOT THIS ONE IN THE BAG, GOKU!

YOU STILL SAY SOME PRETTY WEIRD THINGS, GOKU...

MADAME CRONE ?
YEAH ?

PSS PSS PSS

LORD MUTEN-RÔSHI, IS SOMETHING THE MATTER? YOU'VE BEEN AWFULLY QUIET FOR A WHILE...
HMM--...

WHAT ARE YOU WORRYING ABOUT?! GOKU'S INVINCIBLE NOW!! THERE'S NO WAY HE CAN LOSE!!
THAT'S NOT WHAT I WAS THINKING ABOUT...

THE MASKED CHAMPION'S VOICE SOUNDS VAGUELY FAMILIAR... I HAVE THE FEELING THAT I'VE MET HIM SOMEWHERE BEFORE...
BUT I JUST CAN'T REMEMBER THE DETAILS... I CAN SENSE THAT HE HAS AN AURA OF GREAT POWER, HOWEVER....

WHAT?! POWER?! ***HIM***?!
MY CRONE OF A SISTER WOULDN'T HAVE SO MUCH CONFIDENCE IN HIM UNLESS HE WERE A MASTER.

YOU'RE KIDDING.
HE DOESN'T ***LOOK*** MUCH LIKE A MASTER.

OH, *HO*, ***HO***!! SO THAT'S WHAT YOU HAD IN MIND!!

WELL, WELL.... *HEH HEH HEH*... THIS WILL BE QUITE A TREAT!
ARE WE GONNA FIGHT OR NOT?
?

BOW

GO, GO, GOKU!!

DON'T LET YOUR GUARD DOWN!!

DON'T WORRY!! I'M GONNA WIN!!

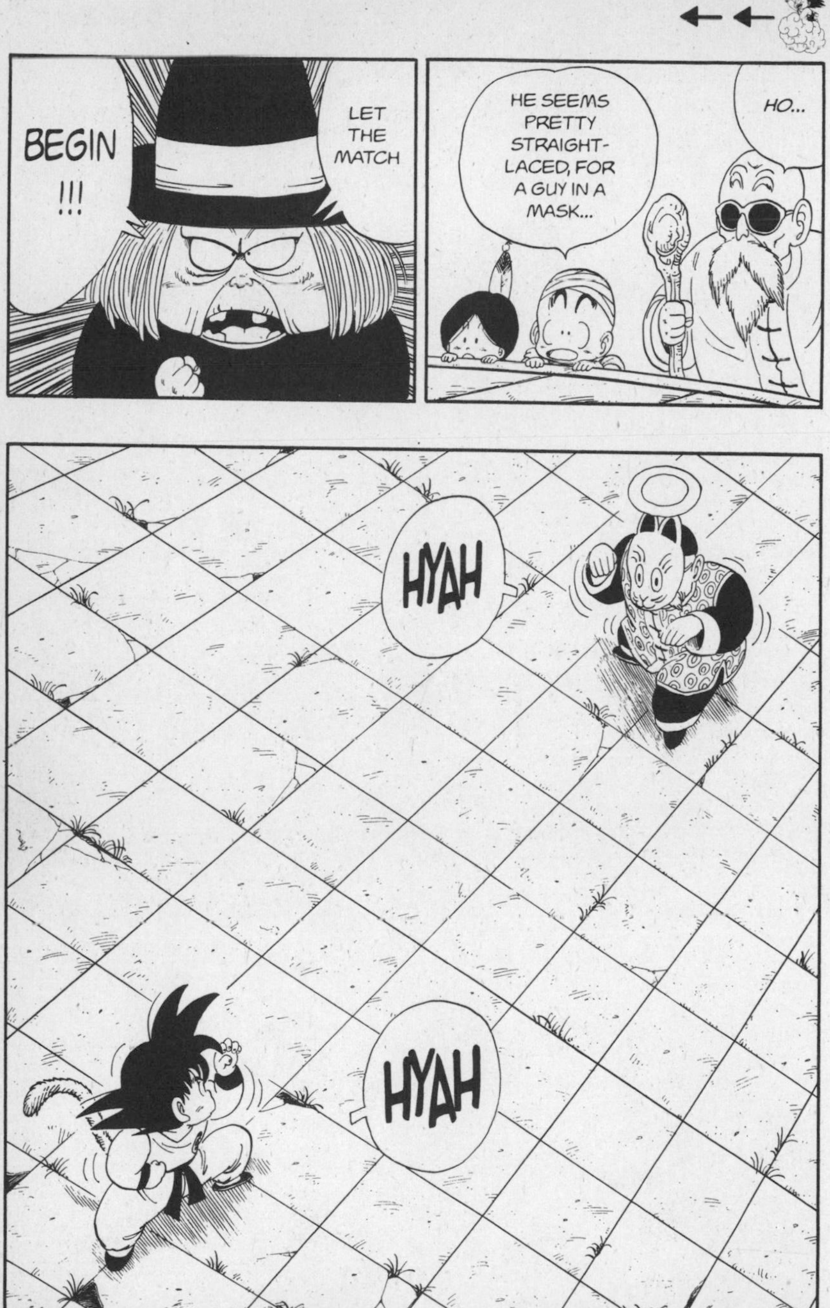

HO...
HE SEEMS PRETTY STRAIGHT-LACED, FOR A GUY IN A MASK...

LET THE MATCH
BEGIN !!!

HYAH

HYAH

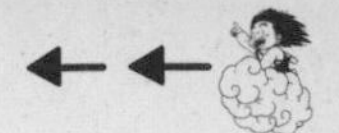

HMM...
GULP

THIS ONE...
...WILL **NOT** BE AN EASY MATCH... !

HE'S... STRANGE.
HIS POWER'S TOTALLY DIFFERENT FROM THE OTHER ONES ...!!

ATTACK !
OKAY !!!

TAH !!!!

DMM

!!

TSUO !!!!

VNNN

UGH !!!

PWAH

URRRGH...
!!
GRRRR...
!!

GWRRRRR

TWAH

VOOOM

!!

BWAK

HMPH
!!!

VOM

ffp

GONG

NEXT: The Masked Man's Identity

Tale 106 • Strong vs. Strong

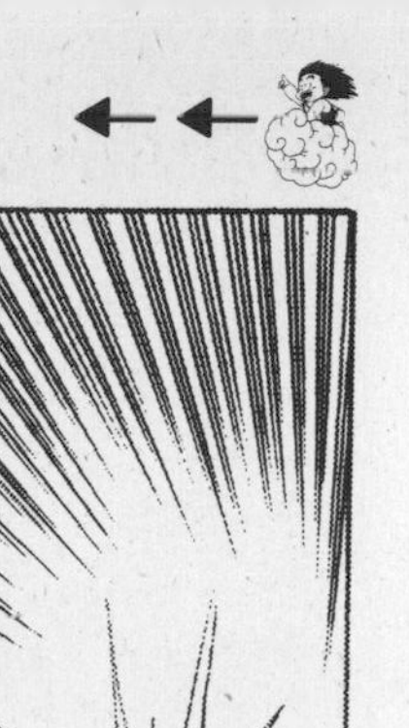
DOMM

PWAPF
GLOK
PAP
ZDD

BWOK

GRAB
OH!!

BAMM

VOONN

W-WAAH!!
HE TOSSED HIM UPWARDS!! WHAT'S HE PLANNING TO DO?!

SKOOSH

OH !!!
Z-BOOM
GWOGG
GUH !!!

COLORING PAGE

Use pretty colors to make us look cool!

AAAARGH !!!!

B-KOOM

N-NO !!!!

THAT MUST HAVE HURT.

HO HO HO

WHAT?!
OH !!!!
BOOM

KIIIN

OH !!
TOP

BOMM
TOH !!!

VWOOOO

CLENCH

DBOM

HUH
?!

!!

TOP

HEH HEH HEH...
WOW, YOU'RE STRONG! THIS IS EXCITING!

WHAT KIND OF TRAINING DID HE GET ?!
HE TOOK MY KICK AT FULL FORCE... !!

WELL THEN... PERHAPS I SHOULD TOSS IN A SURPRISE, EH...?
SSS

HUH ?!

KA
ME

WHAT ?!

N-N- NO WAY... !!

...!!!

IT'S A TRICK... RIGHT... ?!
Y-YOU'RE KIDDING... !!
?

HA

REALLY ?!
HUH ?!
ME

HA!

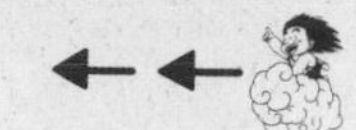

ZOOSH

NEXT: Who, Kame-Sen'nin? Who?

Tale 107 • To Win By a Tail

I'M OVER HERE!
THAT WAS AWFULLY DEFT...
...DODGING MY KAMEHAMEHA WITH A SPLIT-IMAGE ILLUSION AND ESCAPING TO THE SKY...

WH-

WHAT THE ?!

HA...

ME...

DON'T TELL ME...

YOU KNOW THE KAMEHA-MEHA TOO?!

HWOOO

HA--
!!!!

VVVV

!!
VWOOM

DAM

PAP

SLUMP

FWAH
NN...
NNH...
!

YAH--
!!!

ZOOD
GYAA
!!!!

AIEEE--...
HEY, DO YOU SURREN-DER?

SH- SHOOT !!!

IF YOU DON'T SAY "UNCLE", I'LL GIVE YOU THE FINAL BLOW!!

YEAH !!
HE WON !!

HO HO HO HO...

HUH ?

GNNG

SSHP

OH... !

GYUUU
HEY !!

OH NO !!
IF YOU SQUEEZE GOKU'S TAIL, HE GETS WEAK!
WHAT ?!

PANT
PANT
WOBBLE WOBBLE
FLOP

WHAT?! I DIDN'T EVEN KNOW THAT!!
HIS WEAK SPOT... IS HIS TAIL?!
NOW THAT YOU MENTION IT... YOU'RE RIGHT !!

IT'S AS IF HE FIGURED IT OUT...
I THOUGHT PU'AR, THE GYÛ-MAÔ'S DAUGHTER, AND I WERE THE ONLY ONES WHO KNEW ABOUT IT, BUT...

...
HE REALLY IS A MASTER... TO BE ABLE TO SPOT THAT KIND OF WEAKNESS ON HIS OWN...

HO... YOU'RE CARELESS... !
I-I LET MY GUARD DOWN...

TEE HEE HEE! THE TABLES HAVE TURNED, HAVEN'T THEY, LAD?!
YOU HAVEN'T BEEN TRAINING YOUR TAIL, HAVE YOU ?!!

THAT'S IT...!! HIS TRUE IDENTITY *IS*...!
WELL, WELL... THAT WAS THE FURTHEST THING FROM MY MIND!

IT *ISN'T* THAT HE FIGURED OUT GOKU'S WEAK POINT...
HE *KNEW* ABOUT IT ALREADY!
WHAT ?!
WHAT DO YOU MEAN ?!

B-TAM

TAKE THAT !
BOM BAM

PIIP
PIIP

SNEER
UGGH... N-NO WAY...
WELL--DON'T YOU THINK YOU SHOULD BE THE ONE SURRENDERING ?

WE DID IT!!!
THE BRAT'S WEAK POINT IS HIS TAIL!!!

WHEN WE FOUND OUT THAT THE MONSTER LAD WAS GATHERING DRAGON BALLS AGAIN, I DIDN'T KNOW WHAT WE COULD DO...
BUT THE GODS HAVE *NOT* ABANDONED ME!!
THE *REICH PILAF* WILL REIGN SUPREME!

THE DRAGON BALL THAT I KEEP IN THIS SPECIAL CASE CAN NOT BE DETECTED BY RADAR.
HOWEVER, WITH OUR SATELLITE DRAGON BALL RADAR...
...THE SIX DRAGON BALLS THAT BRAT TOOK PAINS TO GATHER ARE AS GOOD AS IN OUR GRASP!

AND FOR MY NEXT COURSE... *THE WORLD*!
WHY WAS I AFRAID OF *HIM*?!!!

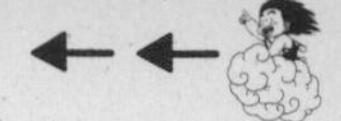

ZWOOM
ALL RIGHT!!! LET'S GO STEAL SOME DRAGON BALLS!!!

BASH

YOU'RE A STUBBORN ONE, AREN'T YOU? YOU STILL WON'T BEG FOR MERCY?
UH-UH... DUMMY...

IT'S NO USE! HE'LL BE FINISHED!
HEY!! HOW COME HE KNEW ABOUT HIS TAIL BEING HIS WEAK POINT?!!

SNAP

WHOOOSH

IF YOU DON'T SURRENDER SOON, YOU'LL DIE!

WHAT ?!

***NEXT*: Son Gohan**

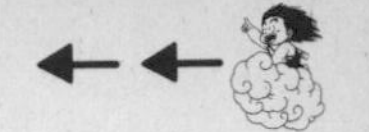

OWW!!

OH, HO--!! GOKU'S LOST HIS WEAK POINT-- !!!

YEOW--!
YEOW--!
SH-SHOOT...!! HIS TAIL SNAPPED OFF...!!

H-HE'S GOKU'S DEAD GRANDFATHER... ?!
...SON GOHAN...
WH-WHAT ARE YOU TALKING ABOUT!! I THOUGHT HE DIED A LONG TIME AGO!!

OH, YES, SON GOHAN IS QUITE DEAD, INDEED...
SEE -- THERE'S A HALO FLOATING OVER HIS HEAD!
TH- THEN HOW... ?

OWWWW-- ...!!
H-HOW DARE YOU TEAR OFF MY TAIL-- !!

...

CROUCH

NOW I'M
MAD--!!!!

UNCLE.
I LOSE.

HO HO HO...

HUH ?!

H-...
HE WON... ?

WELLLL...
I GUESS THAT'S IT...

YOU'VE GOTTEN QUITE STRONG, GOKU...
YOU'VE TRAINED WELL... MOSTLY.
H-HOW DO YOU KNOW MY NAME... ?!

BUT IT SEEMS YOU'VE BEEN SLACKING ABOUT TRAINING YOUR TAIL... I THOUGHT I WARNED YOU ABOUT THAT...

...

Y... YOU...
YOU DON'T MEAN... !!

MY MY... HOW EMBARRASSING...
IT TOOK YOU THIS LONG TO FIGURE IT OUT?

THAT'S RIGHT, LAD...
...IT'S ME.

GRAND-
PA...
!?

G-
GRAND-
PA...

GRAN-
PA--
!!!!
HA
HA
HA
!!

GRANPA
GRANPA
GRANPA
!!!
VOOM
WHOA,
LAD
!!
C-
CAREFUL
THERE
!!

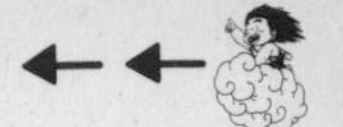

WAAH-- GRANPA-- !!
SILLY BOY, THERE'S NO NEED TO CRY!
OH DEAR, SON'S CRYING... !
NO SURPRISE... STRONG AS HE IS, GOKU'S STILL A KID...
SNIFF

SORRY ABOUT YOUR TAIL...
IT LOOKED LIKE YOU HADN'T OVER-COME YOUR ONE WEAKNESS, SO I THOUGHT I'D TEACH YOU A LESSON...
I GUESS I DON'T QUITE KNOW MY OWN STRENGTH...!

IN ANY CASE, YOU REALLY ARE A MARVEL! I NEVER THOUGHT I'D BE THE ONE TO LOSE!
DID YOU RECEIVE TRAINING FROM LORD MUTEN-RÔSHI?
YUP !

MASTER RÔSHI, LONG TIME NO SEE.
YES, IT'S BEEN A WHILE... EVEN I DIDN'T REALIZE IT WAS YOU AT FIRST.

GRANDPA, WHEN DID YOU COME BACK TO LIFE?!
OH, I HAVEN'T COME BACK TO LIFE.

THE ESTEEMED ALL-SEEING CRONE...ELDER SISTER OF OUR LORD MUTEN-RÔSHI...CAN TRAVEL FREELY BETWEEN THIS WORLD AND THE NEXT.
AND SO SHE SCOUTS DECEASED MARTIAL CHAMPIONS AND BRINGS US BACK HERE TO FIGHT MATCHES...FOR QUITE A NICE SALARY, I MUST SAY!

THEN DOES THAT MEAN YOU CAN COME LIVE WITH ME AGAIN?!
ALAS... NO.
IT DOESN'T WORK THAT WAY. I CAN RETURN TO THIS WORLD FOR ONLY A SINGLE DAY.
YOU MEAN THE TWO OF YOU MEETING TODAY WAS A TOTAL COINCIDENCE?!

HECK NO! MY BIG SIS CAN READ THE FUTURE! SHE **KNEW** WE'D BE COMING TODAY...DIDN'T YOU?
HEH HEH HEH-- OF COURSE!

GOHAN ASKED ME TO LET HIM KNOW IF A LAD WITH A TAIL CAME BY.
I HAD NO IDEA YOU WERE HIS GRANDSON!

I'VE BEEN CONCERNED ABOUT HOW GOKU WOULD DO... I NEVER DREAMED HE'D BE TRAINING UNDER YOU, LORD MUTEN-RÔSHI.
THANK YOU SO MUCH. NOW I CAN RETURN TO THE OTHER WORLD WITH NO WORRIES.

BY THE WAY... HAS GOKU BEEN TRANSFORMING INTO A GIANT MONKEY?
PSS PSS
DON'T WORRY--EVER SINCE I DESTROYED THE MOON, IT'S BEEN VERY PEACEFUL!
PSS PSS

HEY? WHAT ARE YOU GUYS WHISPERING ABOUT?!
OH!! *UH...* NOTHING! NOTHING AT ALL!!

HEY, HEY!! I'VE GOT SOMETHING NEAT TO SHOW YOU, GRANDPA!!
HMM?

HEH HEH HEH... LOOK, I'VE STILL GOT IT!!
HO! I REMEMBER PICKING UP THAT LITTLE BAUBLE A LONG TIME AGO...
EH?! WHY ARE THERE ALL THESE OTHERS?!

THAT BALL CHANGED SON GOKU'S LIFE FOREVER!!

OH?

...SO THAT'S THE STORY.
MY, MY...
SO THAT'S WHAT THIS IS...! I HAD NO IDEA...

SUCH A SURPRISE, MASTER RÔSHI... THAT ONE OF YOUR STUDENTS WOULD BE OBSESSED WITH WOMEN...
OH, SHUT UP!
TH-THANK YOU SO MUCH !!

AND NOW ...
SINCE YOU WON...AS PROMISED, I'LL DIVINE FOR YOU !
TOP

WELL THEN.
I SHOULD GET GOING BACK TO THE WORLD BEYOND.

GRANDPA, DO YOU HAVE GO BACK SO SOON?!
IT MAKES ME VERY HAPPY TO SEE YOU COMING ALONG SO WELL, GOKU.

I HOPE MASTER RÔSHI AND ALL OF YOU FRIENDS OF GOKU WILL CONTINUE TO LOOK AFTER THE LITTLE RASCAL!

MADAME CRONE, THANK YOU VERY MUCH... TRULY.
SURE. TAKE CARE!

I'LL BE LOOKING FORWARD TO SEEING AN EVEN MORE GROWN-UP GOKU IN THE DISTANT FUTURE!
YUP !!

WELL THEN! SEE YOU ALL AGAIN IN THE NEXT WORLD... SOONER OR LATER!
...
...
...
YEAH... I CAN'T WAIT...

I'M GLAD YOU'RE WELL...
...FOR SOMEONE'S WHO'S DEAD, AT LEAST...
HA HA HA!

BYE BYE, GRANDPA!! I'M REALLY GLAD I GOT TO SEE YOU!!
DITTO!

GOOD-BYE...
TAKE CARE...

POOF

G'BYE...

GRAND-PA!
WHEN MY TAIL GROWS BACK I'M GONNA TRAIN IT TOO, AND I'LL BE A WHOLE LOT MORE STRONGER!!
IF YOU GET ANY STRONGER THAN YOU ARE NOW, *MY* REPUTATION'S GOING TO BE HISTORY!

NEXT: Pilaf's Master Plan!

COLORING PAGE

Use pretty colors to make us look cool!

TITLE PAGE GALLERY

These title pages were used when these **Dragon Ball** chapters were originally published in Japan from 1986 to 1987 in **Weekly Shonen Jump** magazine.

Tale 99

The Five Champions

Akira Toriyama
鳥山明
BIRD STUDIO

WE WON'T LOSE TO ANYONE!

SHOW 'EM THE FIST OF THE WOLF FANG!

Tale 100
Battle of the Bleeders

Akira Toriyama
鳥山明 BIRD STUDIO

<Son Goku's Team>		<Baba Uranai's Team>
Kuririn •	Kuririn loses	• Count Dracula
Pu'ar / Upa •	Count Dracula loses	• ?
		• ?
Yamcha •		• ?
Son Goku •		• ?

Dragon Ball

Akira Toriyama

鳥山明

BIRD STUDIO

YAMCHA'S READY! BUT WHO'S NEXT?

Tale 101 • The Devil's Cesspool

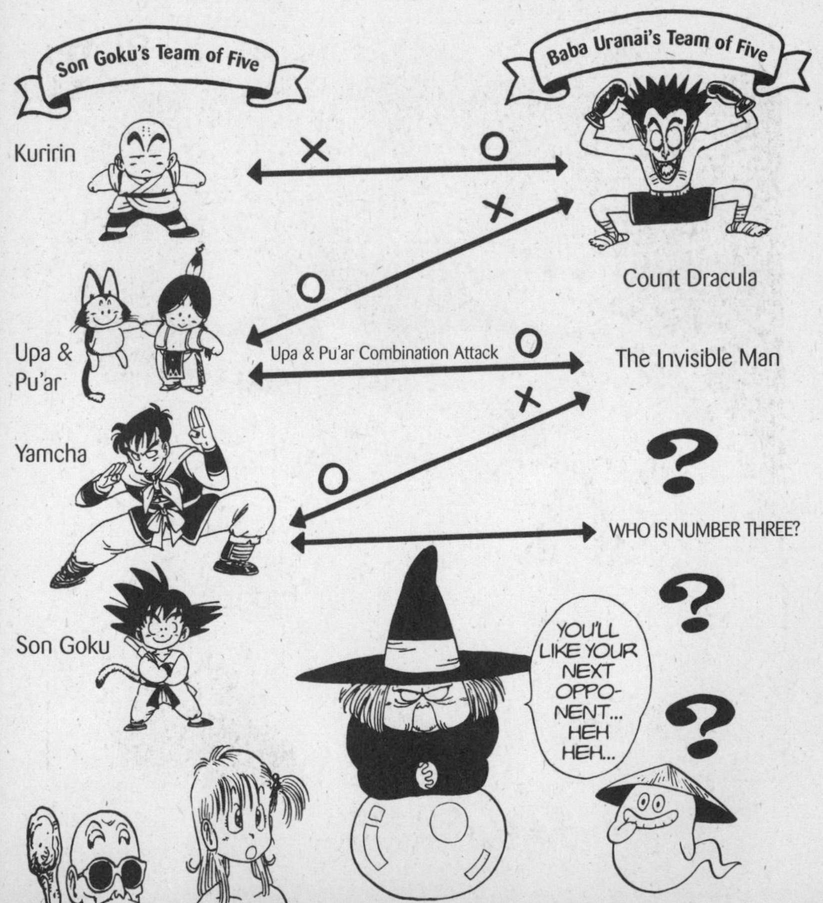

FIGHT ABOVE THE DEVIL'S CESSPOOL!

Tale 102 • Goku at the Plate!

Akira Toriyama
鳥山明 BIRD STUDIO

THE MONKEY VS. THE MUMMY!

Tale 103 • The Power of Goku!

NOBODY'S GONNA BEAT ME UP!

Tale 104 • The Beam of Evil

Akira Toriyama
鳥山明
BIRD
STUDIO

DRAGON BALL
Tale 105 • The Last Champion
Akira Toriyama
鳥山明
BIRD STUDIO
WONDER IF HE'S TOUGH...?

1987

SPECIAL COLOR SECTION FOR 1987!

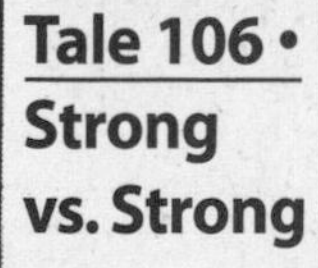

Tale 106 • Strong vs. Strong

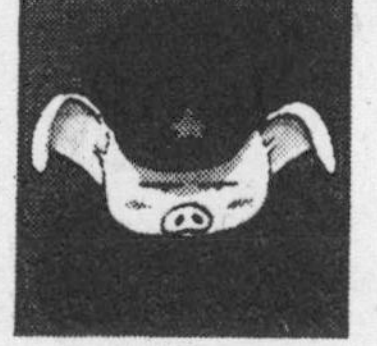

THE DECISIVE BATTLE!

Tale 108 • Son Gohan

DRAGON BALL

Thanks to all of your great support, ***Dragon Ball*** has reached its third year of serialization! We are extremely grateful, so to thank everyone, I, Akira Toriyama, will sign several telephone cards! For three weeks, five winners a week will be selected to receive cards. Only fifteen winners will be selected, total, but everyone should enter this drawing!

• Draw your favorite ***Dragon Ball*** character (only one character, please!) on a postcard. Don't forget to include your name, address, and age.
• Next, we will randomly choose five lucky winners and send them signed telephone cards with a sketch of Bulma!
• Send postcards to: Shueisha, Dragon 2, ***Shonen Jump***, P.O. Box 66, 101-91 Tokyo-to, Chiyoda-ku, Kanda-kyoku, Japan.
• Entries will not be accepted after February 2, 1987. Winners of this drawing will not be eligible for other contests in this week's issue of ***Shonen Jump***. Prizes will be sent directly to winners.

[Editor's Note: This contest expired in 1987, so please don't send any postcards!]